A Daily Devotional

Everything Good

GOD IN THE QUARANTINE OF 2020

MONICA GARNETT

Zyia Consulting
Illuminate & Transcend

Everything Good: God in the Quarantine of 2020

Zyia Consulting
Book Writing & Publishing Company
www.nyishaddavis.com
nyisha.d.davis@gmail.com
678-881-5983

To contact the author about speaking at your event go to
garnettmonica62@gmail.com

Unless otherwise noted, all Scripture quotations are taken from
www.blueletterbible.org

ISBN: 9798686911406

Printed in the United States of America.

"And I am certain that God, who began the good work within you, will continue his work until it is finally finished on the day when Christ Jesus returns."

Philippians 1:6 NLT

Dedication

This devotional book is dedicated to my husband, Maurice, who has always encouraged me on this journey. You are the prophet, priest, provider, prayer warrior, and Man of God whom God has placed in my life. To my son Rome, don't ever give up on your dream. God has a plan for you. I pray that you will learn to walk with Him and trust Him on the journey. To Joycelyn, my oldest daughter, who has always been a joy to me, my coach, and entrepreneur, thank you for inspiring me just to write. God has his hands on you. Continue to allow Him to bring his visions to pass in your life, the wisdom to work the vision, and always seek Him first. Rachel, your spirit gives evidence to the meaning of your name - lamb, gentle, meekness, humble. I pray that you will come to know and love Him with all your heart, mind, soul, strength, and put no one and nothing before Him. Your business Geekylychic and fashion sense are off the chain! I love your style, be yourself in all you do, God is right there with you. And to you, Jada, as you read this book, know that God cares. He knows all about you. Run into his loving, open arms. He is waiting to hold you. Don't allow worry to grip your heart concerning anything. God has blessed you with many gifts. Use your gifts to bring Glory to God. To all of my grandchild, I pray you will come to know God and all that He is.

Acknowledgment

It has taken me quite some time to write, "Everything Good." There were times when I doubted my abilities, myself, and my purpose. I can go back as far as 2011 while attending a biblical studies program, at the Geraldine Marvel Miller Wright Institute, I told my instructor I had a book in me. I graduated from that institute knowing I was an evangelist and teacher. I knew there was something that needed to be expressed and taught. I kept putting off writing because I believed my only platform was upon a stage in front of a crowd; I never wrote the book. I repeated similar words at the end of 2017. Six years later I started writing, only to be distracted another year by taking my eyes off God. I started looking at my husband, my children, my grandchildren, my job, and my church family. I was distracted by everything.

I attended yet another biblical institute to further understand this hunger and thirst in my soul; longing to draw closer to God. It was after graduating from the Impact Bible Institute in June 2019, at Grace Christian Church in Sterling Heights, Michigan that I knew I just had to do it. I began to "write the vision and make it plain on tablets, that he may run who reads it." (Habakkuk 2:2 NKJV) and trust God. I sincerely believe God places people in your life at just the right time. He set before me this team of individuals who labored with me to put in black and white what God had laid on my heart.

My Sincere Thanks

I thank God in all His Divine inspiration given to make this vision come to pass. He deserves all the Glory for His guidance and wisdom, inspiring me to write the vision. My parents, for without you, there would be no me. Thank you for your love and your teachings. My husband, you have the fruit of patience, and I am so grateful for that and for all the love, laughter, meals, times we've shared, and for your support. I am always thankful.

Nyisha D. Davis, my niece, graphic designer, friend, and "The Encourager" who helped me put this devotional together step by step, week by week, and month by month. She helped bring my book cover to life. I am blessed to have you working with me as God knows graphic design is not my gift. The best is yet to come for you. The Holy Spirit has brought us together; the love and insight you brought to the table were priceless. You are indeed a gift from God.

Joycelyn Thurmond, Rachel Henderson, and Jada Garnett, my cheerleaders. Thank you for reminding me of my gifts. In so many ways, you inspired me to keep it moving. Your energy, your vibe to create is contagious. It made reaching this goal a pure delight.

Monique Lazard, my editor, you spent your time editing and proofreading this devotional time and time again working to make it as accurate as possible.

And To every apostle, prophet, evangelist, pastor, teacher, and layperson I encountered on my journey who planted seeds of the truth of the Gospel of Jesus Christ in my life, thank you.

Reflections

"He who dwells in the secret place of the Highest Shall abide under the shadow of the Almighty," I will say of the Lord, "He is my refuge and my fortress; My God, in Him I will trust."

Psalms 91:1 NKJV

God Almighty

Do you know the God who is Almighty? Do you believe the Almighty God will hear and answer your prayers? The Almighty Sufficient One is our place of rest. He will keep you safe from present dangers and troubles. He will protect you from outside influences by placing a hedge of protection around your home and your family. The present chaos around the world today does not change who Almighty God is. Surely we can trust in Him. We must rest in His promises to save us from deadly diseases and to keep us under His wings of protection. His faithfulness is our shield. We have no need to fear the riots at night or the plagues by day. Though it is evident that thousands are falling every day, it will not come near us.

In the book of Genesis, we hear God tell Abraham who he is, *"I am Almighty God."* (Genesis 17:1 NKJV) He is Almighty God, the God of more than enough. The Almighty has sent His angels to surround you and protect you. When the children of Israel came to the Red Sea, not knowing how they would get to the other side, while their enemies were hot on their trail and gaining ground. They began to fear and cry out, "What are we going to do?" The Almighty stepped in and made way for His children with a dry path to the other side. He held the waters of the sea until they all passed through the waters. These same waters collapsed together and drowned their enemies when they pursued God's children.

When the Almighty's children cried for food, He fed them bread from heaven. When His children were thirsty, the Almighty provided water from a rock. When the people of Israel were engaged in war in the land of Canaan and needed daylight for their victory, Almighty God heard Joshua's prayer and stopped the rotation of the universe for His people. They overcame their enemies because the anointing power of Almighty God was upon them. He is God, and He is All-Sufficient. In response to God naming Himself *"Almighty,"* Abraham assumed a posture of repentance. That is the only adequate reply to the Almighty Sufficient God, Abraham fell on his face, and so should we. (Genesis 17: 1-3)

> Jesus himself declared, *"Anyone who has seen me has seen the Father!"* He told the Jews, *"I tell you the truth, before Abraham was even born, I AM."*
> John 8:58, 14:9 NLT

You may not have seen God, but you can feel His presence. You may not have seen God, but you will know when His Spirit is leading you. You may not have seen God but you will know when He has saved, healed, delivered, and protected you. Trust and believe in the All-Sufficient, Almighty God for everything you need today! He is the God of your right now! Get excited about what the Almighty can do in your life. Ask, and the doors will be opened to you, seek, and you will find.

Worship: You Know My Name - Tasha Cobbs, Boasting - Lecrae and Anthony Evans, & The Lord Is Able - John P. Kee

Scripture Reading: Exodus 13, 15:11, & 17:6, Jeremiah 29:13, Psalms 17:8, Zechariah 2:8, Galatians 4:6-7, Revelation 1:8, Isaiah 9:6, Psalms 91 &100, 1 Peter 1:16, & 1 John 1:9

Prayer: Almighty God, I/we exalt you today; you deserve all the glory, all the honor, and all the praise. Holy and righteous is your name. You are the first and the last, the beginning and the end, and there is none like You. Forgive us for our sins and cleanse us of all unrighteousness. We recognize your sovereign power. It is in you that we live, move, and have our very being. Without you, we are nothing. We need you Almighty God. We are calling on Your name.

"Moses built an altar and called it The LORD is my Banner. He said, Because hands were lifted up against the throne of the Lord, the Lord will be at war against the Amalekites from generation to generation."

Exodus 17: 15-16 NIV

"Be strong and courageous. Do not be afraid or terrified because of them, for the Lord your God goes with you; he will never leave you nor forsake you."

Deuteronomy 31:6 NIV

God is My Banner

God, have you left us? God, are you still here? Have you asked these questions lately? There is a spiritual war raging all around us, and we all have a role to play. We have quarantined from the deadly global invisible presence of the coronavirus disease for months. Before its disturbance is under control, another deadly virus attacks God's people again. The deadly presence of global racial injustice, police brutality, and systemic injustice continue to corrupt our land, yet this one is not invisible. Black men and women are being murdered. Cellular videos and news reports have captured these occurrences over and over again. Recent killings of Ahmad Arbury, Breonna Taylor, and George Floyd ignite the fire. Will it ever stop?

People respond differently to the same situation. These unjust acts of murder and discrimination are being carried out by some who were sworn in to serve and protect the people. The cries of pain, oppression, discouragement, and grief can be heard across the nations. People are dying and people are crying because of the long history of racism and corrupt police brutality in America. Protesters fill the streets of our nation and around the world, to be heard, seen, and to make a lasting change. The awakening of our nation is in full bloom.

Their voices can be heard throughout the night. We will not be an outcast because of the color of our skin. Black lives matter; enough is enough. The blindfold has been taken off, and many from other cultures and nations join the fight for equality and justice for all. We shall overcome someday. Every chain is broken. Yet the enemy keeps trying to continue with these senseless killings. The blood will be on their hands. Whatever a man sows is what he will reap. Get your minds and your hearts ready for battle as the globe fights against the spread of the coronavirus, racism, as well as, social injustice, and police brutality.

As children of God, we do not wage war as the world does. The weapons we fight with are not carnal weapons, but mighty weapons in God that pull down strongholds. We have the power to bring down everything that attempts to exalt itself against the knowledge of God by bringing every thought into obedience to Christ Jesus. Like the people of Israel, who used the double-edged sword, had the advantage over their enemy as Moses held his staff in the air; we also have the same advantage. The battle was won. God gave them victory.

God is our banner. Keep your eyes on the Lord; our circumstances do not defeat us. We trample on serpents and scorpions; we keep the enemy under our feet when we hold up the Word of God. God will rescue us from evildoers and protect us from those that devise evil plans in their hearts and stir up war every day. (Psalms 37) He will remove those from the land whose acts are evil and whose hands are filled with acts of violence.

It is through Jesus that our spiritual battle is already won. We will still face struggles, but if we have faith and obey God, He will go before us. It does not matter how many people the enemy has brought against us. God will fight for us, just like he fought for Deborah and Barak in the book of Judges. Barak's army against the enemy was only ten thousand, while Sisera, their enemy's army, had a multitude of fighters and nine hundred iron chariots. But God fought for Israel, and they overtook the enemy. (Judges 4:1-24)

Because God is our banner and protection, we also have the privilege to come boldly before the throne of grace to seek wisdom. He alone can lead, bless, protect, and give us supernatural victory over evil forces. Do not let your hearts be troubled, and do not be afraid of your enemies that seem too big to conquer.

"We are more than conquerors."
Romans 8:37 NKJV

Keep your eyes on the Lord; watch him stand fast in the faith, be brave, and be strong. God has set up a banner for the nations. Acknowledge God in your battles. No matter what inward or outward battles you are fighting, God is fighting with you in every situation. Honor the Lord, call on Him, and He will meet you right where you are. God will show up and show Himself strong on your behalf.

Worship: Victory – The Clark Sisters, This Battle is Not Yours - Yolanda Adams, Worth Fighting For - Brian Courtney Wilson, & Close Close - Marvin Sapp

Scriptures Readings: Exodus 17: 8-15, Isaiah 5:26, Zechariah 9:16, 1 Corinthians 16:13, Songs of Solomon 2:4, Isaiah 11:12, Hebrews 4:16, Deuteronomy 31:6, 8, Psalms 27:1-3, Exodus 33:14, Isaiah 40:21-25, 2 Corinthians 4-6, Luke 10:19, & John 14:27

Prayer: Father God, You are my light and my salvation, whom shall I fear? Deliver me from all who are violent, whose hearts devise wicked plans. I bind all fear and intimidation that would come through racism or brutality in the name of Jesus. Let all those be exposed who hold unjust violence in their hearts in the name of Jesus. Let racism and deadly diseases cease in the nations. Though wars break out against us, we will be confident and trust in You. Help us to humble ourselves and call on You so that you may forgive our sins and heal our land in Jesus mighty name I/we pray. Amen.

"But blessed is the one who trusts in the Lord, whose confidence is in him."
Jeremiah 17:7 NIV

"For you have been my hope, Sovereign Lord, my confidence since my youth."
Psalms 71:5 NIV

God is My Confidence

Is your life progressing? Who or what are you putting your confidence in? When your confidence rests in God, His promises will lead you to blessings. God is our confidant. He is here for us, and we can receive courage and confidence to face our circumstances every day, we can entirely rely on him. We can be confident in our salvation, our prayers, ourselves, our purpose, and even in our trials. You belong to Him, and He belongs to you. Rest in that truth. Our salvation comes with knowing that God loves us so much that He gave His only begotten Son, with the reassurance that whoever believes in Him will *"not perish but have everlasting life."* (John 3:16 KJV) The death of Jesus was only the beginning of a new life.

Do you know God has your best interests at heart? When faced with something that is beyond our abilities, God wants us to respond with a yes I can do this, and put our trust in Him, knowing He has equipped us with everything we need. Don't be distracted by the loud screams of the enemy in your ear telling you, "It's not going to happen." Hold on to your confidence in God, and watch what God will do for you. Our confidence in God will get us through grief, anger, and fears. With the help of the Holy Spirit, we can understand how to apply the Bible's wisdom to our situations.

Our confidence in answered prayers comes from knowing if we ask anything according to the will of God; He hears us. (1 John 5:14 NKJV). When we pray to our Heavenly Father saying "Father I know you can do this;" we remind Him of His word and promises to us. God expects His Word to be exhibited in our lives. Therefore, increase your prayer life and proclaim His Word. God hears you, and he will answer. Don't put your confidence in the flesh as the apostle Paul wrote, *"those who worship God in spirit rejoice in Christ Jesus, and have no confidence in the flesh."* (Philippians 3:3 NKJV)

God may cause us to fail at something we know we are capable of doing, just to keep us humble and asking for His help. Similarly, God will cause us to succeed at something we had no knowledge of and no business trying. Our faith should not be in our wisdom or the sense of man, but rather in the power of God. We have confidence in our purpose because we understand that God began a good work in us and has promised to carry it out until the day of Christ Jesus. (Philippians 1-6) The only one who can stop your dream(s) from becoming a reality is you.

We have to be confident that God will bring us through attacks on our health, our family, our finances, and our careers. Don't listen to bystanders giving you negative feedback or gossip. Don't look at how big your enemies are. Keep your eyes on the Lord and see His vision for you.

"Greater is he that is in us than he that is in the world."
1 John 4:4

"Trust in the Lord with all your heart; do not depend on your own understanding. Seek his will in all you do, and he will show you which path to take."
Proverbs 3:5-6 NLT

Song: Everything Will Be Alright – Isaiah Templeton, Erica Campbell - Praying and Believing, & Walter Hawkins - He's That Kind of Friend

Scripture Reading: John 3:16, 2 Corinthians 5:8, 1 John 5:14, Psalm 34:15, 1 Corinthians 2:5, Proverbs 3:26, Psalms 27:2 – 3, Hebrews 3:6, Psalms 28:7, Deuteronomy 7:18, Psalms 44: 3, Jeremiah 17:7, Psalms 71:5, & Proverbs 3:5-6

Prayer: Father God, you are my confidence. In you, there is no failure. You're an all-wise God. Thank you for Jesus and the promise of everlasting life and for keeping your ears open to my prayers. I ask you to keep me humble and thankful at all times. I pray in the name of Jesus that I will clearly hear the call that you have on my life. Holy Spirit, help me to stay on track and not distracted with unnecessary tasks, people, or places. Give me the confidence to wait on your perfect timing. Teach me to live as I go through this day. Cover me with the belt of truth and the breastplate of righteousness. Guide my feet with the gospel of peace and protect my head with the helmet of salvation. Grant me your wisdom in every situation I face today. My confidence is in you, no other hope I know. In Jesus' name, I pray. Amen

"The Spirit of the Lord is upon me, for he has anointed me to bring Good News to the poor. He has sent me to proclaim that captives will be released, and that the blind will see, that the oppressed will be set free, and that the time of the Lord's favor has come."

Luke 4:18 NLT

God is My Deliverer

Have you ever judged someone by their outer appearance? I know I have, and if the truth is told, most of us probably do regularly. What thoughts cross your mind when you see the man or woman holding a sign on the corner, the prostitute walking down the street? What about the woman dressed in a flimsy dress coming into the church you attend or the gay couple holding hands while entering the sanctuary? How do you react? The book of Romans tells us all have sinned and fall short of the glory of God. (Romans 3:23 NIV)

Jesus came to deliver us out of our horrible pits and the miry clay we were stuck in and to place our feet on solid ground. We all have a past, yet when Jesus saves us, some of us forget the bondage we were in before He rescued us. We are to spread the good news about Jesus to those that God places in our path. God will give you these opportunities if you ask Him, and even when you don't. There will always be times we can guide people to Jesus, and that's what we are commissioned to do. When we tell people about Jesus, and they later decide they need a deliverer, a Savior, then we have assisted in setting the captives free.

Rahab was a woman of the Bible who I'm sure experienced the stares and judgments of her community. She was a prostitute. I can see her neighbors' looking at her in disgust while children overhear their mother's gossip, laughing and pointing their fingers in Rahab's direction as she walks through town. But Joshua, the leader of God's people in that season, told two spies to go to Rahab's place and hide from the enemy. Rahab had heard the good news of how the Israelites left Egypt in victory and how their God had parted the Red Sea.

When the two spies came to her home, she provided them a way to escape from their enemy. In return, her whole family was kept safe, as God's enemies in her hometown were brought to shame. That night God gave Joshua and Rahab the victory. Rahab believed in the God of Israel, and He delivered her out of bondage. Old things were left behind; all other things have become new. One of Rahab's descendants was David, one of God's appointed kings of Israel. She was also the generational grandmother of Jesus, who is the Savior of the world. God honors faithfulness. He hears your cry. He will deliver you in the time of trouble. He will preserve you and keep you alive.

Don't drag your past into your future! God wants to prosper you; when you accept Jesus as your Savior, He erases your past. Forgive yourself and move forward. The name of the Lord is a strong tower; the righteous run to it and are safe. (Proverbs 18:10 NKJV). Let the Lord be magnified!! He alone is our help and our Deliverer.

Worship: I Almost Let Go – Kurt Carr, Deliver Me & This is my Exodus The Tri-City Singers & Jonathan McReynolds

Scriptures; Luke 4:18, Psalms 40:2, Psalms 40:17, Romans 3:23, Daniel 3:17, Psalms 41: 1-2, Psalms 23, Psalms 46, Psalms 32: 7-8, Isaiah 43: 1-3

Prayer: Heavenly Father, I need you right now, help me to keep my eyes on you and not my problems, the enemy, nor my struggles. I believe that you love me enough to deliver me from all my enemies, and keep me in the midst of trouble. I need your deliverance from the oppressors and depression. I ask you to break every chain of bondage in the name of Jesus. You said you came to open our eyes and set us free. Release your angels to surround and protect me, as well as, my family, friends, neighbors, church family, and people of God. I believe you can do more than I can even think or ask. I'm asking You to speak to me, Lord. Tell me what to do, and how to do it. I need you to deliver me out of this fire in Jesus' name I pray. Amen.

"There remains, then a Sabbath-rest for the people of God; for anyone who enters God's rest also rests from their works, just as God did from his."
Hebrews 4:9-10

Today's Reflection

God is Emmanuel

God is Near – God is With Us

Come into God's presence today, willing to learn and change. God desires to be near you. Most of us have experienced times in our lives when we feel like God is nowhere to be found, we ask for help, but our situation remains the same. We feel as if God is not moving in our timing, and therefore think that God is ignoring us or the sins we have committed are unforgivable. Our prayers have not been answered, and our troubles look bigger than something God can handle. But these are thoughts of deceptions. That is why it is so important to renew our minds daily with the Word of God. God is a very intimate Father. Draw near.

"Don't copy the behavior and customs of this world, but let God transform you into a new person by changing the way you think. Then you will learn to know God's will for you, which is good and pleasing and perfect."

Romans 12:2 NLT

Have you ever tried to complete every task on your to-do-list in one day? I have. It took me years on my journey, and I still have to continually remind myself to relax, take a deep breath, and tell myself this task can wait. Being a follower of Christ requires us to learn to use wisdom and balance into our daily schedule. Prioritizing your time with God will make your day more productive. Practice sitting at His feet before managing the household chores or going to work. I remember the day of my daughter Rachel's wedding we hosted in our home. I was so busy cleaning our house, running around to the Party City store for decorations, the grocery store for food, and preparing the backyard's seating and floral arrangements.

I was so busy to the point where when the guest arrived, and the vows were made, I failed to meet and greet all the guests. My husband, on the other hand, was sitting down, eating, and laughing with everyone. I was so upset with him. I was also so embarrassed when this reality hit me in the face. I had not taken the time that morning to seek God. I put everything in my hands and went to work. I was worried about whether there would be enough chairs and enough food. I was a total mess running around trying to do everything. The word tells us to do just the opposite.

"Don't worry about anything; instead, pray about everything.
Tell God what you need, and thank him for all he has done."
Philippians 4:6 NLT

I believe the story of Mary and Martha, in Luke 10:38- 42, is another excellent example of how God wants His children to spend time drawing near to Him. Take some time to read it today. Martha opened her home to Jesus and immediately started making sure everything was perfect; the food, the seating arrangements, and the cleaning. She was distracted by all that needed to be prepared. But Mary chose to sit at the Lord's feet while He was near. She had joy, peace, and was recognized by Jesus as doing what pleased Him most.

When God whispers your name, and you hear His voice stop whatever you're doing and find out what He wants to share with you. If you have been ignoring His voice, stop! Answer the call. Sit at His feet. Get rid of your old bad habits. Staying busy will not fulfill the void in your soul. Only Jesus can fulfill the desires of your heart. When He calls you, He wants you as much as you need Him. It will require your sacrifice of time, but it will be time well spent. It's for our benefit that we draw near to God while He is near. It is in these times that He will prepare us for whatever we will face that day. Choose what is better, and it will not be taken away from you.

Worship: Name Above All Names - Martha Munizzi, A Great Work - Brian Courtney Wilson

Scriptures: Isaiah 7:14, Luke 10: 38 - 42, Psalms 73:28, Matthew 1:23, Psalms 145:18, Philippians 4:6

Prayer: Father God, let me know that you are near; my mind is racing. I/we ask you to help me set my priorities in order. Holy Spirit, be that comfort to me in this anxious moment, help me to walk in greater fullness of your purpose and your presence. God, you see all, you see me, and are with me. In Jesus' name I pray. Amen.

"Because of the Lord's great love we are not consumed, for his
compassion never fails, they are new every
morning; great is your faithfulness."
Lamentations 3:22 NIV

Today's Reflection

God is My Faithful Father

When you hear the word father, what image comes to our mind? Most likely, it's a male figure. It may have positive or negative emotions connected to it depending on your relationship with your biological father, stepfather, adoptive father, foster father, grandfather, Godfather, uncle or whoever fulfilled that role in your life. Perhaps you grew up without a father figure in the household, and your mother fulfilled both roles. Whatever your specific situation may have been, we have a perception of what we believe a father should do, and what role he should play.

A father is defined as a man in relation to his child or children. Similar meanings for father include bringing into being, bringing into the world, reproduce or beget. (1) Now let's look at God as our heavenly father. He brought us into existence when He breathed the breath of life in us. (Genesis 2:7 NKJV) When we accepted Jesus as our Lord and Savior, He adopted us into his family.

"See what great love the father has lavished on us, that we should be called children of God! And that is what we are!"
1 John 3:1 NIV

Now that's powerful. We are God's children created in His image. Why am I bringing these scriptures out? Because whether you were abandoned or abused in your childhood, God is here to be your Heavenly Father. God is *"a father to the fatherless and a defender of widows."* (Psalms 68:5 NKJV) This is who God is. His arms are always open to receive His children. Even when we feel like we don't deserve His love and forgiveness, He is waiting for us. Even if we commit the same sin over and over again and find ourselves back in a dark bottomless pit, God is waiting for us.

Some of us can relate to being lost and rebellious to the teachings of parents. It is not uncommon for teenagers and young adults to believe their plans are better than following the old-fashioned advice from parents. As a result, many cannot wait to leave their parents' home to live independently. Their idea of living the best life is defined by wasting money on eating out, drinking, smoking, and hanging out with friends. This perception is clouded by selfishness, lust, disrespect, and carelessness. Soon these cycles may lead to fornication and looking for love in the wrong places, leading possibly to paths of darkness, rejection, pain, abandonment, brokenness, and abuse (mental, physical, emotional, and/or sexual).

Like many, I regret some of the choices I made during the years leading up to my adulthood, and came to realize that my parents were right while I was wrong. God allows us to make mistakes in our choices. All the lessons in our lives cannot be learned without some level of difficulty; they are needed to teach us a lesson. For the rebellious child, the scriptures tell the story of the prodigal son. This story tells us about a son who wanted to explore his selfish desires believing his plans were bigger than his earthly and Heavenly Father. He asked his father to give him his inheritance at a young age. Take note of this parable; it does not name the child. The son's name is not prodigal, but his behavior is just that. I believe the word prodigal can refer to any child of God, male or female. The father gave his son his inheritance, and a few days later, his son packed his suitcases and left his father's home.

He traveled to another country and wasted all his money on women and a frivolous lifestyle. Circumstantially, a severe famine hit that land and he had to beg for food because he had spent all of his inheritance. As a result, he found a job working for a citizen of that country who sent him into his fields to feed pigs. He was so hungry that the slop the pigs ate looked appealing. As he agonized in the reality of his actions and hunger pains, he started thinking and came to his right mind.

He said to himself, my father has land with bread and servants. I'm sure he has plenty of leftovers. I'm going back to my father's house. I'll ask him to forgive me, and beg him to allow me to work for him. When the son's father saw him coming, he ordered his servants to get his son the best robe, best jewelry, and the best food. His father threw him a party. He rejoiced at seeing his son return home. He realized his son had come to his right mindset, and God answered his prayers and brought his son back home. (Luke 15: 11-19 NKJV)

For us to attain peace in our surroundings and in our hearts, we need to learn the lessons God is teaching us. When we resist the devil and submit to God, the devil will flee. In this, we have overcome and gained victory. God disciplines us while being a very patient and forgiving Father. Nevertheless, He allows us to make our own decisions. Don't listen to those negative thoughts in your mind that may drive you to make decisions based on how you feel. Believe that you are loved, and God has a better plan for you.

"For I know the thoughts that I think toward you,
says the Lord, thoughts of peace and not of evil,
to give you a future and a hope."
Jeremiah 29:11 NKJV

"It is of the LORD'S mercies that we are not consumed because his compassions fail not. They are new every morning. Great is thy faithfulness."
Lamentations 3:22 KJV

Worship: Great is Thy Faithfulness - Cee Winans, Keep the Faith - Charles Jenkins, & Change Me - Tamela Mann

Scriptures: Genesis 2:7, 1 John 3:1, Genesis 1:27, Lamentations 3:22, Psalms 36:5, 40: 11, 57:10, & 68:5, 2 Thessalonians 3:3, Jeremiah 29:11, Luke 15: 11-19, Proverbs 3:11, 1 Peter 3:9, & James 4:7

Prayer: Heavenly Father, thank you for your love, your compassion, your faithfulness, you have been so faithful in extending to me. I ask you to forgive me for my sins I've had in my life, for those times I have been rebellious, selfish, disrespectful, lustful, without self-control, grumbling and complaining, and for not trusting in the purpose you have for me. For not honoring my father and mother, and not loving You as I should. I repent of my sins. Holy Spirit, I ask you to be in my heart and my thinking, be in my eyes and my seeing, cleanse me of all unrighteousness, and help me extend that same love, compassion, and faithfulness to others who cross my path each day. In Jesus' Name. Amen.

"And we know that in all things God works for the good of those who love him, who have been called according to his purpose."

Romans 8:28 NIV

Today's Reflection

God is Good

Do you see the many reasons to be grateful in these uncertain times? We often hear the word good. We say the food is good, it was a good movie, the weather is good, it's a good day to do this or that, that's a good looking man or a good looking woman. We even go around saying I'm good. However, when such a word is used so frequently, it can become so familiar that we grow immune to the depth of its meaning. Today let us consider what good entails. There is no amount of money, car, career, house, man, woman, boy, girl, or anything else that can compare to the goodness of the Lord.

Reflect and refresh yourself in the goodness of God's presence today. God is the wellspring of all goodness and all good things. His goodness consists of salvation through Jesus Christ; we cannot earn it, nor do we deserve it. God freely gives His goodness; that includes His favor, grace, mercy, patience, and kindness. His purposes are always pure. Our earthly parents, grandparents, spouses, family, and friends give good gifts to us. How much more does our Heavenly Father enjoy giving good gifts to those who ask Him! (Matthew 7:11) He loves us with an everlasting love and draws us with unfailing kindness. God is good and can only do good.

"Every good and perfect gift is coming down from the Father of the heavenly lights, who does not change like shifting shadows."

James 1:17 NIV

In the short story of the rich young ruler found in Mark chapter 10, the ruler addressed Jesus as *"Good Teacher."* So, Jesus said to him, *"Why do you call me good? No one is good but One, that is, God."* (Mark:10: 17-18 NKJV). From the beginning of His creation, God looked at what He did and saw that it was good. Yes, God complimented His own good works! Scripture reminds us to think about those things which are excellent. What occupies your thoughts throughout the day?

Philippians 4:8 (NKJV) says, *"Finally, brethren, whatever things are noble, whatever things are just, whatever things are pure, whatever things are lovely, whatever things are of good report if there is any virtue and if there is anything praiseworthy- meditate on these things."*

God shows us His goodness daily by the many good things that add to our comfort and enjoyment. Let us not take God's good gifts for granted. When you have established an intimate relationship with the Lord, then you will know what it means to taste and see that the Lord is good. Embrace the goodness of

God every day. Not just when things are going according to our plans. Put on the whole armor of God and reject every thought that does not line up with the word of God. Focus on the goodness of God today because He is Good!! All the time. Jesus told the disciples, *"In the world, you will have tribulation; but be of good cheer, I have overcome the world."* (John 16:33 NKJV)

Worship: You are Good - Greg Kirkland, Who You Say I Am - Hillsong Worship, & For My Good - Todd Galberth

Scriptures: Psalms 33:5, 34:8 & 84:11, Jeremiah 29:11-13, Proverbs 22:6, 2 Corinthians 4:17, John 16:33, James 1:17, Jeremiah 31:3, Genesis 1:10, & Ephesians 2:8, 6:10

Prayer: Father, God, thank you for being so good to me/us. I ask you to give me a thankful heart that is always aware of your blessings, both big and small. Let Your blessings fill my life and come upon my family and friends. I will give to Your work, and it will be given to me; good measure, pressed down shaken together and running over in the name of Jesus. You've given me the free gift of salvation, love, mercy, grace, kindness, and good time and time again. Help me be mindful of all the good gifts You share from your heart every day and not take them for granted. Help me/us to intentionally fix my/our gaze on You and your eternal gift, In Jesus' name. Amen.

"Bless the Lord, O my soul: and all that is within me, bless His holy name! Bless the Lord, O my soul, and forget not all His benefits: Who forgives all your iniquities, Who heals all your diseases, who redeems your life from destruction, Who crowns you with lovingkindness and tender mercy, Who satisfies your mouth with good things so that your youth is renewed like the eagle's."

Psalms 103: 1-5 NKJV

"I will bless the LORD at all times; His praise shall continually be in my mouth."

Psalms 34:1 NKJV

Today's Reflection

God is My Healer

Are you able to look beyond the doctor's report, and trust God's promises of joy and healing? Sometimes the only thing to slow us down is a severe health issue or death. Why do we wait for calamity to slow our pace? The world draws us to move forward in our careers and agendas. We try to make the most of every hour and every minute. But our bodies need daily rest for healing on the inside.

We read numerous stories in the Bible about how Jesus went from town to town, healing every person who came to Him. Because He is the author and finisher of our faith, it is God's will that we are healed. When they whipped Jesus and nailed Him to the cross, every manner of sickness and disease was defeated. Jesus paid the price for our healing, and He wants you to be whole. Have you ever doubted God could use you because of you messed up? Have you ever asked God to use you? You may have heard the saying "be careful what you pray for." I remember asking God to use me for His Glory, I believe my testimony of how God healed me will encourage someone today.

In February of 2006, I heard those dreadful words "You have

breast cancer." I sat on the doctor's table devastated, alone and afraid. I was an emotional wreck. My first selfish question to God, as I recall, was, "Why me? I have eight other sisters. Why me?" I was angry at God, angry at the physician's laid-back attitude as she spoke of my alternatives and how I needed to have surgery right away. I walked out of that office in tears that day knowing it would be the last time I would see her face and that I would never go on the operating table with her standing over me.

Often when we hear bad news of unexpected sickness, that we can't logically explain, we may wonder if God is still with us or cares. God cares, and He is with us. He wants his children healthy and prosperous in mind, body, and soul. There is power in knowing that God wants you to succeed and prosper.

While I never doubted that God cared. The truth be told; at that time, I did not have control over my emotions. That was something I had not learned to do. But, I believe God knew I had enough faith to believe He would heal me, and He was right. Learning to wait and trust Jesus is a vital part of our journey. We must learn to face our trials with endurance. *"Endurance develops strength of character, and character strengthens our confident hope of salvation."*
(Romans 5:4 NLT). I'm not trying to make the process of my healing sound easy. It was one of the most challenging trails I have ever confronted. But God's spoken word coming from

your mouth, along with prayer and praise, are the keys to your healing. One of my favorite scriptures that brought me through that season was Psalms 103: 1-5. That word blessed, healed, and delivered me. It is by His stripes that we have our healing.

There are steps we need to take to live healthy and prosper. Many times we know what we need to do, yet we do not practice what is best for us. For example, overeating, fast foods, sugary drinks, chips, chocolate ice cream, cake, and cookies are not the healthiest choices for living. Watching television for eight hours and scrolling social media most of the day are not the best way to spend the time God gives us. We forget that our bodies belong to the Lord, and we are living sacrifices here to do His good pleasure. Our physical, mental and spiritual health are all essential. We should make the changes we know we need to make to live healthy lives that will allow us to do great works for the Lord and watch Him do great works for us.

God healed my body in October of 2006, which was nine months after the diagnosis. I did not undergo chemotherapy or radiation, and I give God all the glory for that!! I've been cancer-free for fourteen years. I am healed! Today God still gives me opportunities to pray for others who have been attacked by this deadly disease. Your experiences, both good and bad, are opportunities for you to share your story and give God the glory He deserves. Let everybody know about what God has brought you through as a testimony to overcome our enemies. God is our Healer. If you're going through a test of trust that involves healing, trust that God is able. Be open to following His divine instructions of wisdom as you go through it with Him. He has made known His benefits for you, and you can trust Him at His word. Jesus touched the eyes of the blind men and said, *"according to your faith, let it be to you."* (Matthew 9:29 NKJV)

Worship: Won't He Do It – Koryn Hawthorne, I See Miracles – Jekalyn Carr, As Long As I Got King Jesus - Vick Winans, & Keep the Faith - Charles Jenkins,

Scripture: Psalms 30:4-5, 34: 1, 103, & 139: 13, Jeremiah 17:14, Isaiah 53:5, 3 John 1:2, Revelation 11:12, & Matthew 9:29

Prayer: Father God, thank you for the faith you have placed in my heart to believe you are willing and able to heal me. I declare I will not die but live and declare your goodness. Sickness and disease have no power over me. May I never forget all of your benefits. The blood that was shed on Calvary has healed every organ in my body, bringing life, healing, and health in the name of Jesus. I thank you that my faith makes me righteous in Your sight. I declare that no weapon formed against me shall prosper, and the blood running through my veins is free from sickness and disease. In Jesus' name. Thank you for keeping me safe in Your arms.

"Great is our Lord, and mighty in power; His understanding is infinite."
Psalms 147:5 NKJV

God is Infinite

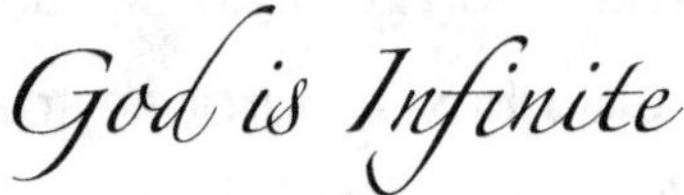

Are you aware of how beautiful life is in God's Presence? In this reflection, I want you to spend time praising God for who He is. The eyes of the Lord are in every place. Our God is infinite. He has no restrictions of space, boundaries, and He never runs out of resources. There is no limit to His creative abilities or His power. The earth is His footstool. He is all-knowing, everywhere present, and all-powerful. None can compare. He knows the number of hair on our heads. He is sovereign over every facet of our lives. He calls the stars and planets by name, while astronauts rocket into space to discover what He has created. Everything is exposed, naked, and open to the eyes of God. Nothing is ever hidden from Him.

"The heavens declare His Glory, who can see their end? The earth is the Lord's and everything in it, the world, and all who live in it; for he founded it on the seas and established it on the waters."
Psalms 24:1-2 NIV

God is faithful. Therefore, He never leaves His children or

His creation. He loves us, created us, and has put great potential in each of us. We are fearfully and wonderfully made in the sight of God. God has a purpose to fulfill in and through you. We are under His reign. His creation of the human race speaks of His creativity, power, authority, and infinite wisdom.

The chaos around the world we are living in right now God has already foreseen. He knows what you need before you even ask Him. We can trust and entirely rely on God, knowing He holds the power of the world in His hands. He has the perfect plan for His children in His timing. With God, all things are possible.

Do you know what your assignment is from God? Underneath all our ashes of sin is the beauty of the Christ-like person God created you to be. You are unique. You are the work of God's hands. He is the masterful Potter who molds us and shapes us into our purpose. Can anyone discover the depths of God? Can you do any amount of research to discover the limits of the Almighty or comprehend His infinite perfection? Who is like the Lord? Nobody.

"The Lord has made bare His holy arm, In the eyes of all the nations; And all the ends of the earth shall see the Salvation of our God."
Isaiah 52:10 NKJV

Worship: Awesome - Charles Jenkins, How Great is Our God - Chris Tomlin, Tasha Cobbs - For Your Glory

Scriptures: Isaiah 52:10 & 63:12, Psalms147:5, Deuteronomy 10:14, Jeremiah 18:4, & Proverbs 16:9, 19:21

Prayer: Heavenly Father, we exalt you today. For your Glory, I will do anything. Show us Your Glory. You are all-powerful, all-knowing, and always present. We thank you for your beautiful creation. Thank you for creating us. Let the Glory of the Lord fill this place. Fill each of us with your Glory; we worship you. Let Your Glory be seen in every nation in Jesus' name we pray Amen.

"And Abraham called the name of the place, the-Lord-Will-Provide; as it is said to this day, In the Mount of the Lord it shall be provided."

Genesis 22:14 NKJV

Today's Reflection

God is Jehovah

What do you need from God today? Who do you turn to for the fulfillment of your needs?   Whatever your need, Jehovah will meet it. His covenants with His children are never broken. When we need provision, we call Him my Jehovah - Jireh, our Provider. (2) When storms arise, we call on Jehovah - Shalom, the Lord my Peace.(3) When we don't know which way to turn, we call the Lord to be our Shepherd. (4) Jehovah is the God of all the earth. In Him, we have everything we need. In our weakest moments, Jehovah is our strength. In times of temptation and sin, we need Jesus, our Savior. When we feel lonely, He is our friend. When we are in a battle, we need Jehovah - Nissi to lead us into our victory. (5) No man can meet our every need - only Jehovah God can, and He manifested who He is through the person of Jesus Christ.

God manifested himself to us in countless ways throughout his word. When He told Abraham to take his son, his only son, and sacrifice him as a burnt offering Abraham obeyed God. When Abraham was about to sacrifice his son, God sent an angel to tell him not to do it. God provided a ram caught in a bush to sacrifice instead of his son Isaac.*"And Abraham called the name of the place, The-Lord-Will-Provide."* (Genesis 22:14 NKJV) God is Jehovah Jireh.

We have evidence of how Jesus calmed the raging storm when he spoke to the waters. A calmness overtook the waters and they were stilled. He gives peace to any situation. He is Jehovah Shalom. When David was faced with the giant Goliath and Saul, the King who tried to kill him, Jehovah Nissi was there to guide and protect him. When the Samaritan woman went to draw water from the well, Jesus offered her *"living water"* because she was drowning in her sins. (John 4:10 NKJV). Jesus is the God of our salvation. He is the *"same yesterday, today, and forever"* (Hebrews 13:8 NKJV) He remains faithful to His word. Jehovah, God, cares about your innermost needs. He wants you to talk to Him about every need you have. Declare His word and believe it in your heart. God is everything you need! Reflect on and believe in Jehovah to meet all your needs today.

"You will also declare a thing, and it will be established for you;
so light will shine on your ways."
Job 22:28 NKJV

Worship: Great Are You Lord - All Sons and Daughters, What a Beautiful Name – Hillsong Worship, Victory Belongs To Jesus - Todd Dulaney, & God Provides - Tamela Mann

Scriptures: Philippians 4:19; Genesis 22, Isaiah 54:17, Nehemiah 8:10, Luke 6:17, Matthew 4:24, Mark 3:7-12, John 4:1-11, & Exodus 15:26

Prayer: Father God, You are my Power, my salvation, my provider, my strength, and guide. Thank you for your saving grace and provision. Thank you for healing me when I was sick, making away when I didn't see a way out of my troubles, and for bringing peace to my mind when times were hard. Holy Spirit, don't let me forget that You are the answer to my every need. Keep me from all distractions today so that I can keep my eyes on what You are doing and all you have done in my life in Jesus' name I pray, Amen.

God is My King

Are you allowing the things of this world to aggravate you? Have you not known, heard, or been told what God is able to do? God sits above the circles of the earth, and we look like grasshoppers before Him! He diminishes rulers to nothing, and makes judges absurd and useless. God removes kings and puts others in position. Leaders often make decisions that affect multitudes of citizens without a thought of what it will cost us in the future. But in the world we live in, the destruction is far from a harmless parable. Some leaders have misused their authority by jumping over others in swarms, leaving people without food, water, healthcare, and the homeless without shelter.

God is greater than the leaders of our nations. He is not a Democrat or a Republican. He is the Creator, King of Kings, and Lord of Lords. High above all the leaders of this earth. Jesus is the greatest King of all times, sitting at the right hand of God. Jesus is Lord! Do not fear. God controls the events of our world. Take some time to read through the short events in the Old Testament and the Proverbs. This is where we find the importance of having leaders who lead in the right direction, and you will see the problems that come when leaders make bad decisions that lead God's people in the wrong direction.

In the Old Testament, we see the one thing good leaders had in common; they did what was pleasing in the sight of the Lord. Throughout the scriptures, whenever kings pleased God, there was peace in the land. The same is true for the measure of an evil king. He does what is evil in the sight of the Lord, and there will not be peace but instead plagues, riots, protests, and wars in the land. This is the same for our lives. When we do what is pleasing to God, we have peace in our souls. Read what God told the people what having a king would be like in 1 Samuel 8:6-18.

The people of Israel wanted a king so they could be like everybody else. God allowed them to choose a king. He told Samuel, *"Do everything they say to you, the Lord replied, for it is me they are rejecting, not you. They don't want me to be their king any longer."* (1 Samuel 8:7 NKJV) Often when given the opportunity to vote, we insist on replacing leadership positions by choosing who we want and not choosing the one that is pleasing to God. Even when officials have been placed after I voted, I have never agreed on every decision they made while in office.

Nevertheless, we are all subject to rulers and those in authority because God has appointed them. We are instructed to pray, obey, speak evil of no one, intercede, and give thanks for all who are in authority. Submit to God's way of doing what's right. Humble yourselves and pray. Allow God to be your King every day. Jesus is Lord!!!

Let us worship our King, *"Lift up your heads, O you gates! And be lifted up, you everlasting doors! And the King of glory shall come in. Who is this King of glory? The Lord strong and mighty, The Lord mighty in battle. Lift your heads, O you gates! Lift up, you everlasting doors! And the King of glory shall come in. Who is this King of glory? The Lord of Host, He is the King of glory. Selah." (Psalms 24: 7-10 NKJV)*

Worship: Take Me to the King - Tamela Mann; King of Glory - Todd Dulaney & The Master's Calling Deborah Joy Winans

Scriptures: 1 Samuel 8:1-21, Isaiah 40:23, Matthew 27:11, Revelation 19:16, 1 Kings 10:23 & 11:1, Psalms 24:7-10, 2 Chronicles 1:8-10, & Titus 3:1

Prayer: Father God, I will place my trust in you when choosing who is to lead our nation. I will not lean on my understanding, power, and might in your hands. You put leaders in position. Help me, Holy Spirit to obey and be submissive to those who rule over me. Help me to pray, intercede, and give thanks to those who are in authority. I realize you know the future and what is best for me. Help me to choose those who are living a life that is pleasing to You and walk according to Your Word. In Jesus' name, I pray. Amen.

"If I could speak all the languages of earth and of angels, but didn't love others, I would only be a noisy gong or a clanging cymbal. If I had the gift of prophecy, and if I understood all of God's secret plans and possessed all knowledge, and if I had such faith that I could move mountains, but didn't love others, I would be nothing. If I gave everything I have to the poor and even sacrificed my body, I could boast about it, but if I didn't love others, I would have gained nothing. Love is patient and kind. Love is not jealous or boastful or proud or rude. It does not demand its own way. It is not irritable, and it keeps no record of being wronged. It does not rejoice about injustice but rejoices whenever the truth wins out. Love never gives up, never loses faith, is always hopeful, and endures through every circumstance."

1 Corinthians 13:1-7 NLT

Today's Reflection

God is Love

Is the love you give real love? If I had to name a person I want to keep on loving me, it's Jesus. The first time I heard a preacher say he loved God more than his wife, I didn't understand how that could be possible. When I accepted Jesus as my Lord and Savior, I said before the congregation, I just want to understand all this God is love stuff. From that moment on, Jesus has opened up His heart of love to me. Over the years, I have come to understand that the Holy Spirit, within, enables us to walk in the spirit of love, becoming the men and women He predestined us to be.

One day my heart was opened to how wide and deep the Lord's love is. God loves us just as we are; we don't have to pretend because He can see right through our fake. We don't have to worry about putting on our best clothing, making up the outward appearance, or for that matter, pretending to be our best self when we meet Him. No, He already knows all about us. So, you can just be you. Come with all your flaws, weaknesses, weight, at any age. God will love on you like you are the only one in the world. You are the apple of His eyes. (Psalms 17:8 NKJV).

Everyone wants to feel loved, feeling acceptance is pretty popular in twenty-first-century society. No one is shocked when they hear about bullying, homosexuality, or gender identity. These terms have become a part of the world we live in. In the book of Romans, Paul wrote, *"accept one another, just as Christ accepted you, in order to bring praise to God."* (Romans 15:7 NIV). The emphasis is on "just as Christ accepted you."Jesus accepted us while we were sinners, but He didn't accept us like that to keep us that way. He accepted us so that through His loving gift of grace, we might be saved from sin and be able to bring praise to God. We are to love one another as they are, love others enough so that they want to be better so that all lives may bring glory to God.

Have you seen people wearing a cross around their necks? The cross is a symbol of the Christian faith. A symbol of what love looks like. Some people wear it as a pretty piece of jewelry, not fully grasping the depth of love that it represents. The cross represents the most painful method of crucifixion. Jesus was beaten for us and was forced to carry His cross. The soldiers hammered nails into His hands, which increased His pain. Then the cross was lifted off the ground and dropped into a hole in the ground. Can you imagine how the force from the cross falling into place would tear the flesh? To breathe, He had to push up on his ankles. Jesus was fully God, but He was also fully man. He felt the emotional and spiritual agony because the nation had rejected Him, and His disciples had denied Him. When He took on our sins, the Father turned away. Yet Jesus willingly offered His blood on our behalf and considered it a joy. No greater love exists than the love of Jesus. The kind of love that God has covers many sins. (Matthew 27.46, 2 Corinthians 5:21, Hebrews 12:2, John 15:13 & James 5:20). Today, reflect on the love Jesus has for you.

"And I am convinced that nothing can ever separate us from God's love. Neither death nor life, neither angels nor demons, neither our fears for today nor our worries about tomorrow- not even the powers of hell can separate us from God's love."
Romans 8:38 NLT

Love is the greatest power. When we love unconditionally, we can change the world through the love of God, love of family, love of all. Learn to love the Lord with all of your heart, soul, mind, and strength; it's what He requires from us.

Worship: 2020 Worship: Reckless Love – Cory Asbury; Your Love - William Murphy, & Jonathan McReynolds - Grace

Scriptures: John 3:16, Romans 5:5, 7-8, & 8:38, Psalms 136: 1-3, 1 Corinthians 13: 4-8, 1 John 4:8-10, 16, Galatians 2:20, Ephesians 2:3-5, 1 John 3:20, Mark 12:30, Jeremiah 31:3

Prayer: Father God, I ask for your wisdom and discernment to recognize the differences between real love and infatuation. Help me to remember true love grows stronger with time and provides for a perfect union with the right man/woman. Teach me to be disciplined in taking the steps I need to take to show Your love in everything to everyone each day and to practice daily living in and walking in Your Spirit, showing Your love wherever you send me in Jesus' name Amen.

"All a person's ways seem pure to them, but motives are weighed by the Lord."
Proverbs 16:2 NIV

Today's Reflection

God is My Motivation

What's your motivation? Why do we do the things we do? There are so many factors that can motivate our behavior to do something about what we believe to be true. For example, when driven by anger, one may act upon the emotion of injustice. When motivated by love, we value an object or person, envy fuels us to want the accomplishments of another, and when we admire things or someone, we value the successes of another.

God knows our hearts. He questions our motivations. In the book of James, the question is asked, *"What causes fights and quarrels among you? You desire but do not have, so you kill. You covet, but you cannot get what you want, so you quarrel and fight. You do not have because you do not ask God. When you ask, you do not receive, because you ask with wrong motives, that you may spend what you get on your pleasures."* (James 4:1-3 NLT)

Whatever drives our motivation to do what we do, we should make sure it is done out of a pure soul. What's a pure soul? I believe a person with a pure soul is someone whose intentions are honest and conscious is clear. It is someone who does things for the joy of doing them, not for merit or status. It is a soul whose decisions come from within the heart, from what the soul believes to be good or right, instead of for attention or self-glory.

Now that you know what a pure soul looks like, let us examine some ways we can obtain a pure heart. We can practice every day with simple acts of kindness, like being good to others on purpose. A good place to start would be in your home; this is our first ministry. God has entrusted us with a family. Let's take good care of our homes, spouses, and children intentionally without complaints. Our workplace is another area where we can practice having a pure soul. By coming to work on time, respecting the organization's mission, our supervisor, department heads, and other employees at all levels. Practice saying good things about the company you work with. Practice keeping your mind free from negative thoughts every day. Practice doing what is right even when no one is looking. Don't gossip about people or intentionally hurt other people. Exercise doing a good deed every day.

I work in an assisted living facility; although this is a challenging position, it's also gratifying to know you have helped several people who could not help themselves. If your motivation for working in this type of capacity is pure, you will have a rewarding day knowing that your labor is not in vain. Scripture tells us to *"Work willingly at whatever you do, as though you were working for the Lord rather than for people."* (Colossians 3:23 NLT) Let us be honest with ourselves. Let's do more of what we really love to do!! Go after what's motivating you with pure motives; examine your heart and soul. Be driven by what you want to do, not by something you feel you have to do. Be motivated to do something that will benefit others, not just yourself. Don't be manipulated by what other people want you to do or be, but rather be guided by your inward desires.

Only the things you do for the Lord will last. The Lord will test our hearts. Have pure motives in your purpose. Allow this to motivate you. Get your motives right. Be the real you!

"Don't be selfish; don't try to impress others. Be humble, thinking of others as better than yourselves."
Philippians 2:3 NLT

Worship: Grateful – Hezekiah Walker & LFC; I Love God - Erica Campbell

Scriptures: Psalms 34:10, Proverbs 18:10, Philippians 2:3 & 3:14, Colossians 3:23, & James 4:1-3

Prayer: God, You have given me everything I need to grow into an effective Christian on this journey. I bear good fruit because of your instructions. I ask you to keep me in your care and guidance as all the gifts that you have given me are cultivated. I ask you to help me stay pure in my motivations in serving you and building your Kingdom. In Jesus' name Amen.

"The Lord is near to all who call on him, to all who call on him in truth. He fulfills the desires of those who fear him; he hears their cry and saves them."

Psalms 145:18 NIV

God is Near

What do you do when it seems like God is not near? We should seek Jesus daily to enrich our relationship with him. He is waiting to answer all your questions about your life here on earth. He wants you to ask Him questions, so go ahead, express yourself! He'll reveal the knowledge you are seeking. As you ask Him questions, be sure to listen carefully to His answers. His answers will draw you closer to Him because He is all-knowing.

God wants us to enjoy our lives with Him while we are here. Accepting Jesus as our Lord and Savior is just the beginning. To grow spiritually mature, we should intentionally draw close to God through worship, prayer, bible study, and applying the word of God to our daily living. When we do that, others will notice the difference. Listen to the whispers of God. He will often whisper to you, inviting you to commune with Him alone. He delights in the intimacy of you, making your request known to Him, and He desires a humble heart before Him. He desires His followers and friends to follow the gentle intimacy of His request.

God loves when you want to be with him to talk about

whatever comes to your heart. He loves when you worship Him and remind Him of everything He is to you. When you acknowledge that He is truly the King of Kings, Lord of Lords, Alpha and Omega, all-powerful, all are knowing, your joy, and your peace, He inhabits your praises and welcomes you in His presence. In Psalms 13, David poured out his heart to God and received his breakthrough when he praised God. So praise Him in the storm.   When we escape from the noise of the day, obey that inner voice, and draw near to God when He summons us to come, there is no greater joy than what He has to share with you in that moment.

When you seek God with your whole heart, you will find Him. It is God's pleasure to hear you sing praises to Him, hear you declare His Word, and to see you grow in faith, learning to trust Him. He loves it, and He loves you. Listen to your spirit and obey those promptings. Do what He asks you to do in that moment. If He says, give, then give. If He says pray out loud, then pray out loud. If His spirit leads you to speak in other tongues, then follow His spirit. Learn to laugh and enjoy God's presence while He is near. Be still and know that God is near. Nurture your relationship with Him first. Then all the other things will come together. Pray, talk, sing, and laugh with Jesus. He'll start revealing those secret things to you that you've always wondered about.

"Draw near to God and He will draw near to you."
James 4:8 NKJV

Worship: You Never Let Go - Matt Redman & You Are Here - William McDowell - I Don't Wanna Leave

Scriptures: James 4:8, Psalms 46:10, & 145: 18-19, 1 Chronicles 16:11, Matthew 6:33, & Jeremiah 33:3

Prayer: Father God, I thank you for the whispers that lead me to you. I thank you for drawing me with your love and kindness. Thank you for allowing me to draw near to you. I want to live for you. I pray that you will fill my lips with prayer and praise. Help me to heed to your voice and spend that quality time with you before I get busy doing other things. Help me never to cease praying to you. Allow prayer to saturate my thoughts and actions so that I will be in constant communication with you In Jesus' name. I pray Amen.

"If you love Me, keep My commandments."
John 14:15 NKJV

"Whoever has my commands and keeps them is the one who loves me. The one who loves me will be loved by my Father, and I too will love them and show myself to them."
John 14:21 NIV

Today's Reflection

God is Obedient

Is all your hard work bringing the increase you want? There is an old saying, "No one gets anywhere without hard work." You might say I have done all that I know to do to bring in your harvest. But, even after putting in the labor and time, there is no harvest. What do you do while you wait? What's the one thing that could be holding up your blessing? The one thing that could be holding up your blessing is your lack of obedience. God has told you to do some things that you have not done. Some may skip this page. I get it. But, it's an uncomfortable conversation that we all need to have with ourselves.

We all struggle with surrendering everything to God. Especially when we are so used to working situations out with our intellect and in our timing. Our pride gets in the way, and we don't want to depend on anything or anyone else to come up with solutions for our struggles. Truth be told, God hates pride. The wisest thing for us to do would be to listen and follow the instructions of God. In doing so, we increase our learning of God's ways, so never stop learning. Our relationship with God has to come from the trust we have for Him and obedience in the application of His Word.

When obedience radiates from our lives, it allows us to move forward. We need to learn to trust God when He tells us what to do. We can learn from the lesson Jesus taught Simon in the book of Luke. Simon was a fisherman, he and his crew had spent an unproductive night at sea and were about to call it a day. Jesus came on the scene and told them to throw their nets in one more time. Now Simon was tired, and he probably had some doubt, but he said, *"Master, we've worked hard all night and haven't caught anything. But because you say so, I will let down the nets."* (Luke 5:5 NIV)

If we don't learn to obey God, we will be stuck like a good looking vehicle on the side of the road without gas. When Simon obeyed, he reaped his harvest. They caught so many fish the nets were breaking. When the Master tells you what to do, no matter how many times you have done it before, or how hard you have worked, there is still something for you to do, and that is to obey. We see Jesus in all His glory was obedient to the will of God.

"Let this mind be in you which was also in Christ Jesus, who, being in the form of God, did not consider it robbery to be equal with God, but made Himself of no reputation, taking the form of a bondservant, and coming in the likeness of men. And being found in appearance as a man, He humbled Himself and became obedient to the point of death, even the death of the

cross. Therefore God has highly exalted Him and given Him the name which is above every name, that at the name of Jesus every knee should bow, of those in heaven, and of those on earth, and those under the earth, and that every tongue should confess that Jesus is Lord to the glory of God the Father".
Philippians 2:5-11 NKJV

God's reward for obedience is better than anything you can accumulate here on Earth. As believers, we have been given an assignment from Jesus. He has told us what to do. We are to go into the world and preach the gospel to everybody. It's our job to introduce people to Jesus. It's His pleasure to save them. We are not responsible for how people react to the message about Jesus; all we have to do is be obedient in spreading the word, and allow Jesus to take care of the rest.

"So neither he who plants is anything, nor he who waters, but God who gives the increase."
1 Corinthians 3-7 NKJV

Today, practice being submissive and obedient. Once you start doing things His way, it will become easier. Be consistent. If you do not obey His voice one day, the next day decide to take control. Surrender all, everything, every day, and in every way. I know that's a great challenge, but I also know that we do

what we want to do when we want to do it. We have a Helper--
the Holy Spirit. We can declare we can do all things through
Christ, who gives us strength.

One thing that keeps us from obeying the voice of God is
our excuses. We justify everything we don't want to do,
knowing that what we don't want to do is what is required.
Let's not fool ourselves or be double-minded. A double-minded
person is unstable and should not expect any thing from God.
This type of behavior will lead to laziness and procrastination.
If you don't understand how to do what God is asking you to
do, then continue the conversation with Him and ask Him for
wisdom. He will give it to you. Break the cycle of disobedience
and move forward.

When we walk in disobedience, we are stuck in a place
spiritually until we decide we are sick and tired of being in that
place and ready to move forward. Practice submitting and obey
without delay. Say yes to the Lord, don't fight against His ways
of doing things right. Remember to know what to do, and not
do it is a sin. When we are obedient to the voice of God,
something supernatural happens. Our obedience to that one
little thing will cause a chain reaction of blessing. Not only
blessings for you, but for others that need to hear what you
have to say, in this way, many are saved.

God has a purpose and a plan specifically for you. Your
flesh, on the other hand, is in a battle with your spirit and

doesn't want to obey. Most of us would rather eat, play, shop, sleep, and repeat. But God has equipped you to fulfill a higher purpose. Trust and obey Him. Take that step of faith, *"...faith by itself isn't enough. Unless it produces good deeds, it is dead and useless."* (James 2:17 NIV)

I put off writing this devotional so many times because I did not believe I was smart enough to write a book. I didn't believe anybody would buy it or read it. I did not believe it was the right time to write a book; all these negative lies came against me. I had procrastination so bad it led to self-doubt and depression. I was in that cycle of doing nothing, so I know first hand what it feels like to be stuck. I have been there and done that.

You have value, gifts, talents, and abilities that you have not tapped into, and you won't reach those dreams without following your inner spirit. Obey the Holy Spirit; He is our teacher. Depend on God to see you through to your destiny. Trust and obey. It's the most excellent way.

Worship: Raise A Hallelujah - Jonathan and Melissa Helser & Every Praise - Hezekiah Walker

Scriptures: Proverbs 1:7, John 14:15 & 15:10, 1 John 2:3 & 5: 2-3, Joshua 1:18, 2 John 6, 1 Peter 1:22, Philippians 4:13, & James 4:17

Prayer: Father God, I want to be more like Jesus every day. Thank you for the example Jesus gave us. Thank you for helping me communicate the truth about Jesus to others. I know you desire that none should perish but that all should come into repentance. I pray that Your word will continue to be shared in the uttermost parts of the world in the name of Jesus. Guide me with Your strong arm every day as I strive to get divine excellence in You. Teach me to obey even when it's hard in Jesus' name. I pray, Amen.

"Peace I leave with you; my peace I give you. I do not give to you as the world gives. Do not let your hearts be troubled and do not be afraid."

John 14:27 NIV

Today's Reflection

God is My Peace

Have you ever planned your day out perfectly just to have it completely ruined? The source of the ruin could be your spouse, your child, a friend, relative, co-worker, or that lady with the big hat that sits on your row in church. In times when we lose our peace, we should remember we don't wrestle with flesh and blood but against principalities, powers, and rulers of darkness in the heavenly places. This is the nature of fallen humanity. No man has the power to disturb your peace, but we allow the world's worries and distractions to get into our heads. We open doors of fear and despondency. The thief comes in and steals and destroys our peace. Put on your armor.

When something or someone tries to steal our peace, we have a remedy from our Father. First, we can pray for that person, and we need the Holy Spirit to do this and let God handle it while keeping your peace. Peace comes when we live and give in a spirit of love. To unite with others, we must love them without forcing our love upon them. Imposing our beliefs upon others will not bring peace.

When we have a genuine concern for others, respect their rights and freedoms, and accept them as they are, peace will manifest within the relationship. Who they are and what they do will have a null effect on us. We cannot change anybody. A person has to want change. An unselfish person likes variety, diversity, and change, allowing other people to live their lives, not interfering with them. Choose your peace. Live an unselfish life that recognizes variety and differences as a delightful thing. We are all different. Accept each other's differences.

We will never agree with everyone all the time, but we don't have to lose our peace when we have conflicts. Our hearts should remain at peace. Not that it's always been that easy to get my peace back after a confrontation, but I have grown to recognize when I'm losing my peace. You know the feeling. Your heart starts beating fast, there is a tightness in your stomach, your facial expressions hardened, your voice escalates to hollering, and insults come flying out the mouth. Be careful to control your mouth when you lose your peace. We do not need to say every thought that comes into our minds. Remember, there is *"death and life in the power of the tongue."* (Proverbs 18:21 NKJV)

It may be hard to control your tongue when you are angry, but it is possible. We can't bless people one day and curse them the next day. All people have been made in the image of God. Watch your mouth and choose life, speak life. When signs of anger trigger your spirit, there is plenty we can do, but only one voice we should listen to. Can you hear God? He's speaking to you, even in moments of anger. He'll tell you what to do. For me, He would say, "Be quiet, and do nothing rashly." (Acts: 19:36 NKJV). To me, those words meant don't be troubled.

I knew this was going to happen to you today. I've been waiting for you. I'm here for you. Listening is essential in every relationship, especially the one with God. Now I know when it's time to step away, examine my heart, and try the conversation later when I have had time to think about what's going on in my heart. I make sure I am free from jealousy and selfish ambitions, and in this way, make room for God's peace, which exceeds all understanding. I have also learned over the years not to be wise in all of my opinions, not to fight with harsh words, or evil actions, but rather attempt to live in peace with everybody.

"Blessed are the peacemakers, for they shall be called sons of God." Matthew 5:9 NKJV

No matter what your situation looks like, no matter how much a person may think he or she has power over you, never forget the Lord has the ultimate authority, the utmost power, and the final say in your life.

Today, let's reflect on and practice walking in a spirit of peace. If you realize you need help in this area, I want you to stop right now and ask God to forgive you and to give you a clean heart, take those bad attitudes away and fill your heart with love, joy, peace, gentleness, and kindness. Pray with a sincere heart, and He will answer your prayers. Walk in the spirit and keep your peace.

"But the fruit of the Spirit is love, joy, peace, longsuffering, kindness, goodness, faithfulness, gentleness, self-control against such there is no law." Galatians 5: 16-23

Worship: Patiently Praising - Lowell Pye & My World Needs You Right Now - Kirk Franklin

Scriptures: Matthew 5:9, Proverbs 18:21, John 14: 27, Psalm 34:4 & 27: 1-3, Philippians 4:6, Joshua 1:9, Galatians 5:16-23, Romans 12:18, & James 3:16, 3:4-5

Prayer: Father God, I receive You as my peace today. I ask you to bind the bad attitudes of pride, selfishness, anger, jealousy, and hatred out of my heart in the name of Jesus. I ask you to help me remember to respect the differences of other people. I ask you to help me listen to understand others better and to be receptive to Your voice. I ask you to help me remember that You are the answer to all of my needs. You gladly supply me with peace, strength, salvation, joy, love, guidance, compassion, and companionship, in Jesus' name Amen.

"For just as the heavens are higher than the earth, so my ways are higher than your ways and my thoughts higher than your thoughts."
Isaiah 55:9 NLT

God is in the Quiet

Where do you turn for the fulfillment of your needs? Have you ever watched the news and details of the story that made you gasp for air; the story is so tragic it left you with your mouth hanging open, or so devastating it brought you tears? Or maybe you recently experienced the loss of a loved one, a home, a positive test result of a deadly disease, or experienced rejection. At times like these, you may wonder how God could allow all this pain to come pouring like a flood in your life. Your emotions are on overload, and you may feel anxious, overwhelmed, and without hope. But these are the trials and tribulations that should cause us to run to God, not run away from Him. It's the perfect time to build your relationship with God. The times in which we need to get in our quiet space. A time to seek peace from our restlessness and fearful thoughts.

God is with us in the quiet, even when our world is in a state of confusion and disorder. By spending quality time in prayer and the Word, you will become sensitive to what God is doing in your life. Get away from the chaos, lock the bedroom door, or take a drive to a quiet place off the water. Do whatever you need to do to get your quiet. Once there, you can cry out to

God, talk with Him, and let Him know how you feel. He wants to know how you feel, don't hide what you are feeling. Let it out, don't hold back. We don't need to suffer from an anxious mind or feel trapped by this world as if there were no one to hear our cry for help.

We can talk to God anytime, anywhere, and He will listen. God has ears that hear and eyes that see. He hears our prayers, and He answers them. Most people have experienced tragedies in their lives, but don't always know how to get through it. Before I grew to know how to deal with situations I reacted in anger. I would scream, seek revenge, and cuss out anybody. I took my frustration out on my children, spouse, coworkers, or anyone who crossed my path. These reactions only made the situations worse; and it took me years to gain self-control.

Now I seek Him in prayer on purpose when I don't know what to do or how to handle a shocking situation in my life. God is in the quiet, and we can't hear if we're doing all the talking. After you've cried out to God in your secret place, take a deep breath, inhale, and exhale. Now allow God to have His voice in the matter. He's in the quiet. Once He knows He has your attention, He will lovingly guide you and comfort you in His arms. Understand He does not think on our level. It doesn't matter how many degrees you have; we all need God's wisdom at some point in our lives.

"For just as the heavens are higher than the earth, so my ways are higher than your ways and my thoughts higher than your thoughts."
Isaiah 55:9 NLT

God is in the quiet, and He knows what is best for you. After you spend quiet time listening to Him, it will bring a calmness to your soul, just like He did for David, who faced many shocking circumstances in his life. David said, "Surely I have calmed and quieted my soul, like a weaned child with his mother, like a weaned child is my soul within me." (Psalm 131:2 NKJV) So, I challenge you to do it God's way. Quiet your soul by spending time in the quiet. The benefits are all yours. I hope this is hitting you in a place you know you need to conquer.

"Our soul waits for the Lord; He is our help and our shield."
Psalms 33:20 NKJV

Worship: In Christ Alone - Stuart Townend / Brian Getty & Living Hope - Phil Wickman

Scriptures: Isaiah 35: 3-4 & 41:10, Proverbs 29:25, Psalms 33:20, 38:15, Psalms 5:3 & 131:2 & 1 Timothy 2: 1-2

Prayer: Father God, slow me down and help me get quiet enough to commune with you, resting in your presence so that I can hear Your voice and apply your teachings to my life. Thank you for listening to me when I call out to You. I trust you will answer with exactly what I need. Help me to cherish these quiet moments with You, to not rush this time alone with You, and not neglect these opportunities. Help me to remember that my worth is not defined by my outward appearance, but rather in the inward beauty you provide in Jesus' name. I pray, Amen.

"Let the words of my mouth and the meditation of my heart Be acceptable in Your sight, O LORD, my strength and my Redeemer."
Psalms 19:14 NKJV

Today's Reflection

God is My Redeemer

Have you embraced Jesus as the One, who without sin, took yours so that you could be free? If you have made Jesus Christ the Lord and Savior of your soul, then you are the ransomed of the Lord. You have been redeemed from all destruction. The Hebrew word for "Redeemer is, ga'al which means, to redeem, avenge, revenge, ransom, do the part of a kinsman, to redeem from slavery, to redeem land, to exact vengeance, to redeem (by payment), to redeem (with God as subject, to redeem), to redeem individuals from death."(6) Now that clearly defines what God has done for His people. Because of Jesus' sacrifice on the cross, our redemption and place in God's family are permanently established, and our inheritance is guaranteed.

"Christ has redeemed us from the curse of the law, having become a curse for us (for it is written, "cursed is everyone who hangs on a tree"), that the blessing of Abraham might come upon the Gentiles in Christ Jesus, that we might receive the promise of the Spirit through faith."
Galatians 3:13 NKJV

All is well. Jesus paid it all. In His redemption, we have life and life more abundantly. Read the story in the book of Job that tells of a man who was perfect and upright before God, who went through troubling times in his walk with God. sJob's children were killed, and all his possessions were taken from him, he suffered from a deadly skin disease where boils covered his body. To make matters worse, his wife told him to give up on God and die. But, Job in all his pain never cursed God with his words. He endured the trial.

The painful experiences we live through are not bigger than God. While our trials continue, remember trouble doesn't last always, they are temporary. God has redeemed you from all curses of failure and frustrations that the enemy sends to trap you. There is no need to fear because your Redeemer lives. You can make it through the storm; you can make it through the pain. At the end of the story, God restored back to Job twice as much as he had before. (Job 42:10-12) He'll do the same for you. Job said, "I know that my Redeemer lives And that in the end, He will stand on the earth." (Job 19:25 NIV) The hour of your redemption has come.

Worship: You're Bigger - Jekalyn Carr, To God Be The Glory - Andrae Crouch, It is Well with my Soul - Horatio Spafford, & My Redeemer Liveth - Clark Sisters

Scriptures: Galatians 3:13, Job 1:1-22, 19:25, & 42:10 1 Peter 5:10, Hebrews 4:16, & Psalm 19:14

Prayer: Heavenly Father, I/we thank you for Your redemptive power. You have redeemed me from all my troubles. I/we will rejoice and sing and give you praise. I thank You that I am holy because I have been redeemed. I praise You because I am justified freely by Your grace and by the redemption that is in Christ Jesus. I pray that you will strengthen me through every trial and help me to endure until my change comes. I thank You, Father God, for redeeming my life from destruction and crowning me with love and tender mercies. I thank you, Father God, for redeeming my soul so that I will place my trust in you. Thank you, Father God, for reminding me that I can do all things with Christ Jesus, who gives me the strength, in Jesus' name.

"The Lord has said, "Nevertheless, I will bring health and healing to it; I will heal my people and will let them enjoy abundant peace and security."
Jeremiah 33:6 NIV

God is My Security

How do you find security in life? Are you seeking security from the world or from God? Today's technology is loaded with security measures for our protection. We have a variety of computer software to protect us while online. We have security guards driving around parking lots while we shop at the mall and on our jobs. We invest in home security systems to protect against dangers and threats. We use devices to monitor activity inside and outside our homes, and likewise businesses, to feel safe knowing that our loved ones and possessions are secure. In spite of that, we know that all of the security measures we take cannot guarantee one hundred percent of our safety.

News reports alone show that despite our efforts, occurrences of theft, cyber crimes, missing children, and trafficking continue to happen. So, how can we live in this world not in fear? As God's people, we have a wall of protection around us. We only have to look up. When we lift our eyes to the hills, we understand where our help comes from. (Psalms 121 NKJV) We have to see this with the eyes of our faith so it will manifest in our present lives.

We must believe that Jesus will guard, protect, and defend us, so that we will not be overwhelmed or consumed by danger. This kind of faith can overcome whatever comes your way-and that is all the security that you need. When we recognize that change is inevitable, we are trusting in God and willing to deal with whatever comes our way. Look at the obstacles we face in the world as it is today; crime, cancer, the Coronavirus, children out of school, businesses and restaurants closed, stock exchange unstable, and riots in our communities. Jesus said, *"...In this life, you will have tribulations, but be of good cheer, I have overcome the world."* (John 16:33 NKJV)

Don't let your security be in your possessions, job, money, spouse, or anything else. If you do, you'll be setting yourself up for a big disappointment. Let's be secure enough in who we are and who we belong to. Find your security by looking up at the sun, moon, stars, and remember who made them. Put your trust in Jesus. Breathe with Him and dance with Him. It's a secure way to live.

One of my favorite scriptures is Psalms 91: 9-10 NIV it reads, *"If you make the Lord your refuge, if you make the Most High your shelter, no evil will conquer you; no plague will come near your home, For he will order his angels to protect you wherever you go."*

Worship: Grace - Charles Jenkins, Great is Thy Faithfulness - Thomas Obadiah Chisholm, Trouble Won't Last - Kendrona Lockett

Scriptures: Nehemiah 8:10, 2 Corinthians 12:9, Philippians 4: 12-13, Isaiah 40:29, & Psalms 91: 9-10

Prayer: Father God, I/we pray in the name of Jesus that you will help me to look to you for my security, and my help comes from You. Help me to trust You every day in every way in Jesus' name. Amen.

"Guide me in your truth and teach me, for you are God my Savior, and my hope is in you all day long."
Psalm 25:5 NIV

God is Truth

What will the truth do to you? When you look at your reflection in the mirror, what do you see? We have to learn to be truthful with ourselves first and love ourselves before we extend love to other people. We need to learn to be our own best friend. Take off the makeup. The truth can hurt us, but it can also change us and set us free. The ugly truth about your past or present has to be confronted with the truth of God's word. Let's look deep into our souls and see who we are. We desperately need to know the truth about who God says we are in His Word, which discovers the condition of our souls.

"For the Word of God is sharper than any double edged sword, it penetrates even to dividing soul and spirit, joints and marrow; it judges the thoughts and attitudes of the heart."

Hebrew 4:12 NIV

As we study and meditate on God's truths, they become stored in our minds and our hearts and eventually influence our actions. The Word of God is meant to transform and renew our thinking and cause us to follow biblical principles. The more we think God's way, the more we'll start to look more like Jesus. We'll have the mind of Christ.

So how do you know God's truth? You get in His word and see what He says about you. Make it a habit to affirm yourself every day with the truth of God's Word. When you look in the mirror each morning, speak to your reflection and affirm yourself, "I am a child of the most high God and saved by His grace. I am forgiven of all my sins. I am a new creature in Christ Jesus. I am a part of a royal priesthood, a member of a chosen generation. I am more than a conqueror. I am strong in the Lord. I am firmly rooted, built up, and established in the faith. I am the righteousness of God, fearfully, and wonderfully made." Then point at yourself and say, "I am proud of you. You have come a long way, baby, and I am ready to face this day with you, Jesus." We need to know that we can do all things with Christ Jesus, who gives us the strength, and we are blessed with every spiritual blessing!!

While we are talking about the truth of who we are, we should be teaching our children and our grandchildren the truth about who they are as well. Teach them in the morning, at noon and before they lay down at night. Give them a strong foundation. Keep your face and mind in the word of God. The truth that's revealed to us can set us free. Are you living your truth?

We live in a world where too many people reject the truth of

God's word. There needs to be a change, not a compromise; God offers us a choice. If you've already accepted Jesus as your Lord and Savior, believing and confessing He died on the cross, rose again on the third day and sits at the right hand of God, you have been given the keys to the kingdom. You have been set apart. Keep your standards high and your guard up by staying in the Word of God and memorizing scripture to help you fight against the enemy just like Jesus did. Stay connected to a Bible-believing church and fellowship with them. And don't forget to pray about everything. If you have not accepted Jesus as your Lord and Savior or have backslidden, don't choose to remain in self-righteousness, choose the Truth. Say a prayer of repentance. Ask Jesus to come into your life. Tell Him you believe He died on the cross for your sins and submit your life to Him. He is waiting for you.

As Christians, we have to live in truth and be completely honest about the areas we need to be set free from. We need to walk with a clear conscience and share real stories with those that don't believe so they can have hope and know that God can deliver them out of bondage. Never give up on yourself. Walk-in, your truth, keep asking the Holy Spirit to help you until every area in your life lines up with the truth that is in the word of God. I say again, be true to yourself, learn to love yourself. There is no one just like you either, so walk in the truth of God's mercy.

Our Creator made each of us unique; we all have value. God is ready to use your truth to bring His name Glory. Share your story and bring others to the love and truth of Christ Jesus. Reflect on this, *"Jesus said to him, I am the way, the truth, and the life. No one comes to the Father except through Me."* (John 14:6 NKJV) Know the truth.

Worship: Jesus Loves Me - Trilogy, I Need You Now - Smokie Norful, & Just want to be Happy - Kirk Franklin

Scriptures: John 14:6 & 8:32 & Psalms 25:5

Prayer: Father God, I/we pray in the name of Jesus that you would forgive me of my sins and cleanse me from unrighteousness. Help me to be true to myself, my family, and my friends. Give me the courage to change the things that I can. Father God, renew me and transform me in the name of Jesus. Amen.

"He who descended is the very one who ascended higher than all the heavens, in order to fill the whole universe."
Ephesians 4:10 NIV

God of the Universe

"There remains, then, a Sabbath-rest for the people of God; for anyone who enters God's rest also rests from their works, just as God did from his.
"Hebrews 4:9-10 NIV

Have you stopped and took a moment just to enjoy God's Creation? If the God of the universe felt it was important to rest after His works of creating our earth, then we know it is vital for us to give up our labor and rest at least one day out of the week. Relax and put up your feet. Watch a good movie, read a good book, or take a walk on the beach. We need to refresh ourselves with activities that relax our mind and bodies which make our leisure times more enjoyable and soothe our souls.

God is the Light of the world. The heavens bring forth His glory. He is the Creator of Heaven and Earth; the fullness of His deity. Infinite. The God of the universe. The universe is everything we can touch, feel, sense, measure, or detect. This includes living things, planets, stars, galaxies, dust clouds, light, and even time. Reflect on God, and worship Him, enjoy His works.

I love to watch birds. My favorite is the canary. Often as I prayed, I would ask God to show me He was near with a canary. More than once, when I looked out my kitchen window there was this beautiful canary. That just made my day. I enjoy watching the sunrise and the sunset; it makes a beautiful picture. I like to curl up with a good book and rub my pet while he is cuddled up next to me. I savor the fragrance of sweet perfume or even walking into a room just sprayed with my favorite air freshener.

I like watching the winter turn to spring, how the buds fill the trees and blossom, and how rainy days leave a rainbow in the sky, reminding me of God's promise. I enjoy seeing squirrels running through the yard chasing each other, and watching a family of geese disrupt traffic walking across the street. While taking a road trip, I might encounter the height of the mountains, the wondrous shapes of the clouds, making them visible objects, and pointing them out. I enjoy driving over rivers, bridges, and lakes while glancing down at the waters. I enjoy the pleasures of a five-day cruise across the waters and landing in Mexico.

God's creation is so amazingly beautiful, and I've only seen a fraction of it. Read Psalm 23 today and reflect on David's words "The Lord is my Shepherd, I lack nothing. He makes me lie down in green pastures, he leads me beside quiet waters, he refreshes my soul." (Psalm 23: 1-3 NIV) You don't have to travel far to find a body of water. There is always a living peace that surrounds us when we relax near water and listen to the sounds of water's lapping and rippling waves; it rests our souls and allows us to hear the still small voice of God. Ahh...take a deep breath in and exhale out. In these moments, God will remind us how much He loves us. Reflect on and absorb the beauty around you every day. God is the Creator and Savior of the universe.

"The earth is the Lord's and everything in it; the world and all who live in it; for he founded it on the seas and established it on the waters."
Psalm 24:1-2 NKJV

Worship: Big – Pastor Mike Jr. & Imagine Me - Kirk Franklin

Scriptures: Ephesians 4:10, Hebrews 1:1-3, & Psalms 103:19 & 24

Prayer: Father, I/we come to You in the name of Jesus. I ask you to open our eyes so that we may see You and the beauty of Your creation. The beauty of those who were made in Your image, the beauty of the universe in Jesus' name, we pray. Amen

"Now this, I know: The Lord gives victory to his anointed. He answers him from his heavenly sanctuary with the victorious power of his right hand."

Psalms 20:6 NIV

God Reigns in Victory

What a glorious victory we have in Jesus. I worked on this devotional for several months. The way we live has changed dramatically over these unpredictable times. We are dealing with the uncertainties of COVID-19, and continued racial injustices against African Americans are at the forefront of unrest. People all over the world are looking to God to save, heal, and deliver us. Suffice it to say, what the world needs is Jesus.

He suffered and died on the cross for our sins and for us to live eternally in peace. So despite all that is going on, we can also spend time reflecting on the victory being already won!!! The Lord has delivered us time and time again. Reflect on your past victories, and then look at the many victories God brought His children through in His Word. David was a young shepherd boy, but because he remembered what the Lord had protected him from in the past, he defeated the giant Philistine, Goliath. (1 Samuel 17) Joshua crossed the Jordan River because he took God at His Word. This is the perfect time to reflect and celebrate the death, burial, and resurrection of Jesus Christ who died on the cross and arose from the dead so that we might receive his salvation which includes peace on earth.

In Isaiah 53:4-7 NLT, we see what Jesus endured to save us; *"...But he was pierced for our rebellion, crushed for our sins. He was beaten so we could be whole. He was whipped so we could be healed. He was oppressed and treated harshly, yet he never said a word. He was led like a lamb to the slaughter. And as a sheep is silent before the shearers, he did not open his mouth."* Jesus was humiliated, spit on, slapped, whipped, mocked and insulted, abandoned, and He is the Son of the living God who had done nothing wrong. Yet, He knew the outcome of His journey. He predicted to the disciples His victory when He said, *"and they will condemn Him to death, and deliver Him to the Gentiles to mock and to scourge and to crucify. And the third day he will rise again."* (Matthew 20:19 NKV)

When you feel discouraged about how your life has changed and how we have all been affected in some way by these realities, remember what Jesus did for you. Today reflect on the victorious reign of Jesus; He Got Up, He Lives, He Reigns!!! Let your heart be filled with joy and peace. Jesus Christ is the same yesterday, today, and forever. (Hebrews 13:8 NLT) Our help comes from the Lord. He has given us the victory. Sin's power has already been destroyed for you when Jesus conquered sin, death, and the grave, to give you life more abundantly. We have everything we need in Christ Jesus; salvation, love, joy, peace, forgiveness, victory, and eternal life.

We are victorious!!! Shout Hallelujah; we have the victory!!! Let Jesus know you trust Him, love Him, and are thankful for all He has done for you.

Worship: Break Every Chain – Tasha Cobbs, My God Reigns, & Pull Us Through - Jermaine Dolly

Scripture: Hebrew 13:8, Isaiah 53:4-7; John 10:10, Romans 6:23, & John 8:36

Prayer: Father God, I/we praise You because You reign in victory, You conquered sin, death, the grave, and You reign in victory. As I continue to run this race, I ask you to give me patience and not allow discouragement to block my victory. You are the God of my breakthrough. I pray that you will allow me to be victorious and breakthrough in my finances and my relationships. Allow me to be victorious and breakthrough in my health and healing. Allow me to be victorious and breakthrough in a new level of prayer, praise, and worship You. I/we will always be eternally grateful in Jesus' name. Amen.

"You are the God who performs miracles; you display your power among the peoples."

Psalms 77:14 NIV

God is a Wondrous Way Maker

Are you waking up expecting God's wonder-working power to work in your life? Do you believe in miracles? God longs to make a way out of no way by performing miracles in our lives. When Jesus is around, miracles happen; people get changed, the dead come back to life, the lame speak, the deaf hear, the blind receive their sight, lepers are cleansed, and the Gospel is preached. God's power is going out to bless through us who believe, "...the works that I do he will do also; and greater works than these he will do." (John 14:12 NKJV) God can do "exceedingly abundantly above all we ask or think, according to the power that works in us." (Ephesians 3:20 NIV)

He's a wonder, in my soul, bless His name. He walked on water and opened the eyes of the blind. He departed the Red Sea and caused the enemy to flee. Our souls should glorify Him when we recognize His goodness and all of the times He made a way for us, and all the wonderful blessings He has given us. Arise from the grave of poverty, sickness, doubt, fear, and limitations. The Glory of the Lord is upon us!!! A wonderful future before us. A future of unlimited power to be a blessing to others. Arise and choose to be used by God!!! Our response to the wondrous, miraculous death, burial, and resurrection of Jesus Christ and His daily presence in our lives should make us want to shout and serve Him while giving Him the highest Hallelujah praise. He is perfect in all of His ways, *"...the author and finisher of our faith."* (Hebrews 12:2 NKJV)

His name is Jesus, the name above all names. He is the wonder-working God of wisdom, the Master of miracles, signs, and wonders. His wonder-working power for healing, salvation, and miracles is activated by your faith. Faith is not seeing, but believing confidently in our God, who is the way maker. Reflect on Jesus' wonder-working power today and be used by God. One writer put it like this, *"Who is like the Lord? There is no one like You."* (2 Samuel 7:22) Jesus is our Miracle Working Wonderful Way Maker, He is Good, and He is God!!!

Worship: Way Maker - Leeland, What a Mighty God We Serve - Hezekiah Walker, You made a Way - Travis Green, & King of Kings (He's a Wonder) - CeCe Winans

Scriptures: Psalms 46:1-3, Proverbs 18:10, 2 Samuel 7:22, & Ephesians 3:20

Prayer: Almighty God, I/we thank you for making away when I didn't see a way out. Thank you for the times you provided for me and protected me from dangers seen and unseen. Thank

You, Father God, for being an ever-present help in the times of need when my back was against the wall and you made a way out. When I was tempted to sin, you made way for me to escape. Thank you for your perfect sacrifice on the cross that gives so many eternal life. Thank you. Father, you are good, and your mercy endures forever. In Jesus' name, Amen.

Author's Notes

In closing, I hope that in your day to day reflections that you will see God in His Sovereignty and how we can know without a doubt that Everything is Good. I hope you can see that God is forever faithful from generation to generation. Amid our trials and tribulations, God is there. We live in a sin-filled world. We can't change that, however, what we can change is how we choose to live in it while we are here. It is our God-given birthright to accept His only begotten Son, who is Jesus Christ, as our Savior.

When we receive Jesus, we gain the ability along with access to spiritual weapons we need to fight against the enemy--the whole armor of God. Even in the toughest trials, God can work all things together for good, and turn the impossible into something good for His Glory. God doesn't cause evil to come upon us. He has good plans for all of us that give our future hope. There will be days in our lives where we can't see His love surrounding us, but we can trust that God is watching over his word. He is a loving God. He has promised to give us His beauty for our ashes.

"Because of that experience, we have even greater confidence in the message proclaimed by the prophets. You must pay close attention to what they wrote, for their words are like a lamp shining in a dark place until the Day dawns, and Christ the Morning Star shines in your hearts."

2 Peter 1:19 NLT

Notes

Songs

Tasha Cobbs. You Know My Name. Heart, Passion, Pursuit. Motown Gospel (EGS) 2017; Lecrae and Anthony Evans. Boasting. WOW, 2012. Verity Gospel Music Group, a unit of Sony Music Entertainment. 2012; John P. Kee. The Lord Is Able. Zumba Recording LLC. 2004

The Clark Sisters. Victory. Victory. Motown Gospel (EGS) 2019; Yolanda Adams. The Battle Is The Lord's. Yolanda. Veriy Records 1996; Brian Courtney Wilson. Worth Fighting For. EMI Gospel/Motown Gospel 2015, Marvin Sapp. Close Close. RCA Inspiration Frontline. 2017

Isaiah Templeton. Everything is Going to Be Alright. Tre'Myles Music, Inc. 2018; John P. Kee. The Lord Is Able. Show Up! Zumba Recording LLC. 2004; Erica Campbell. Praying and Believing. Warryn Campbell. My Block Inc. 2019

C Kurt Carr. I Almost Let Go. Verity Records/Legacy. Sony Music Entertainment 2011.

Donald Lawrence & TheTri-City Singers. Deliver Me (This is my Exodus). Provident Label Group LLC, a division of Sony Music Entertainment. 2019; Jonathan McReynolds. Cycles. Make Room. eOne Music. 2018

Martha Munizzi. Name Above All Names. No Limits. Central South. 2006
Brian Courtney Wilson. A Great Work. Motown Gospel (EGS)
2018

CeCe Winans. Great is Thy Faithfulness. Alone in His Presence. Sparrow
Records. 2013Charles Jenkins & Fellowship Chicago. Keep The
Faith. Keep The Faith. Inspired People, LLC 2019. Tamela Mann.
Change Me. Best Days. Tillymann Inc. 2016

Greg Kirland with "The Gospel" Choir. You are Good. The Gospel See It Live
It Spread It. Zomba Recording LLC. 2005; Hillsong Worship. Who
You Say I Am. Capitol Christian Music Group, Inc. 2018;

Koryn Hawthorne. Won't He Do It. Unstoppable. Provident Label group
LLC, a unit of Sony Music Entertainment. 2017; Jekalyn Carr. I See
Miracles. Lunjeal Music Group. 2019; Earnest Pugh. God Wants To
Heal You. Rain On Us. EPM Music GroupLLCc. 2012

Chapter 9 Charles Jenkins. Awesome. Inspired People Music. 2012; Chris
Tomlin. How Great Is Our God. Sparrow Records 2011; Tasha
Cobbs. For Your Glory. Grace. Motown Gospel. 2003

All Sons & Daughters. Great Are You Lord. Integrity Music. 2013; Hillsong
Worship. What A Beautiful Name it is. Hillsong Australia; Capitol
CMG; Sparrow. 2017

Tamela Mann. Take Me to the King. Best Days. Tilly Mann Music Group,
2012; Todd Dulaney. King of Glory. Your Great Name.

Entertainment One US LP. 2018; Joy Winans. The Master's Calling.
The Master's Calling. Malaco Records, Inc. 2016;

Cory Asbury. Reckless Love. Reckless Love. Bethel Music 2018; Kirk
Franklin. Just For Me.Long Live Love. Fo Yo Soul Recordings and
RCA Records, a division of Sony Music Entertainment. 2019;
Yolanda Adams. I Love The Lord. The Preacher's Wife. Arista
Records LLC. 1996

Hezekiah Walker & LFC. Grateful. 20/85 The Experience. Zomba Recording
LLC. 2005; Erica Campbell. I Luv God. Help. Entertainment One
Music. 2015, Jonathan McReynolds. Grace. People. eOne Music.
2020

Matt Redman. You Never Let Go. Beautiful News. Sparrow records/
sixsteprecords.2006; William McDowell. You Are Here. Sounds of
Revival. Delivery Room Music, distributed by Entertainment One
US LP. 2017; William McDowell. I Don't Wanna Leave. The Cry.
Deliver Room Music, Integrity Music. 2019

Jonathan and Melissa Helser. Raise A Hallelujah. Raise A Hallelujah. Bethel
Music. 2019; Hezekiah Walker. Every Praise. Every Praise. RCA
Records, A division of Sony Music Entertainment. 2013;

Featuring Loyell Pye by Fred Jenkins. Patiently Praising. A Project of
Healing. DarkChild Gospel. 2018; Kirk Franklin. My World Needs
You Right Now. Losing My Religion. Fo Yo Soul Recordings and
RCA Records, a division of Sony Music Entertainment. 2016

Stuart Townend and Brian Getty. In Christ Alone. Lord of Every Heart. Integrity Music. 2016; Phil Wickman. Living Hope. Living Hope. Fair Trade Services. 2018

Jakalyn Carr. You're Bigger. The Life Project. Lunjeal Music Group. 2017; Israel and New Breed. Jesus the Same. Jesus At the Center. Columbia. 2012; Clark Sisters. My Redeemer Liveth. EMI Gospel. 2007

Charles Jenkins. Grace. The Best of Both Worlds. Inspired People Music. 2012.

Byron Cage. Breathe. An Invitation to Worship. Sony Legacy. 2005; Keyondra Lockett. Trouble Won't Last. The Heal Reloaded. Bella Dawn Music, LLC Distributed by IndieBlu Music. 2019

Trilogy. Jesus Loves Me. Jesus Loves Me. UAMG. 2020; Smokie Norful. I Need You Now. I Need You Now. EMI Gospel and Chordant Records. 2003. Kirk Franklin. Wanna Be Happy? Losing My Religion. Fo Yo Soul Recordings and RCA Records, a division of Sony Music Entertainment 2015.

Pastor Mike Jr. Big. Live Free. Black smoke Music Worldwide/Rock City Media Group 2019. ; Kirk Franklin. Imagine Me. The Essential. Verity Records/Legacy. Sony Music Entertainment. 2011

Tasha Cobbs. Break Every Chain. Grace. RCA Records, A division of Sony Music Entertainment. 2014; Jermaine Dolly. Pull Us Through. Pull Us through. By Any Means Necessary. 2019

Leeland. Way maker. Better Word. Integrity Music. 2019; Hezekiah Walker &
          The Love Fellowship Choir; What a Mighty God We Serve.
Family   Affair II. Zomba Recording LLC.2004;

Travis Greene. You Made A Way. The Hill. RCA Inspiration, a division of RCA
          Records. 2015; CeCe Winans. King of Kings (He's A Wonder).
          Sparrow Label Third Party. 2008

Translations

1. Bing.com (2020) "father" Retrieved from https://www.bing.com/
     dictionary/father

2. H3070 - Yehovah yireh - Strong's Hebrew Lexicon (YLT)." Blue Letter
     Bible. Web. 4, Aug, 2020. https://www.blueletterbible.org//lang/
     lexicon/lexicon.cfm?Strongs=H3070&t=YLT>.

3. "H3073 - Yehovah shalowm - Strong's Hebrew Lexicon (YLT)." Blue
     Letter Bible. Web. 5. Aug, 2020. httpss://www.blueletterbible.org//
     lang/lexicon/lexicon.cfm?Strongs=H3073&t=YLT>.

4. "H7462 - ra`ah - Strong's Hebrew Lexicon (NKJV)." Blue Letter Bible.
     Web. 5 Aug, 2020. <https://www.blueletterbible.org//lang/lexicon/
     lexicon.cfm?Strongs=H7462&t=NKJV>.

5. "H3071 - Yehovah nicciy - Strong's Hebrew Lexicon (YLT)." Blue Letter
     Bible. Web. 5 Aug, 2020. <https://www.blueletterbible.org//lang/
     lexicon/lexicon.cfm?Strongs=H3071&t=YLT>.

6. redeemer, "H1350 - ga'al - Strong's Hebrew Lexicon (KJV)." Blue Letter Bible. Web. 23 Jul, 2020. <https://www.blueletterbible.org//lang/lexicon/lexicon.cfm?Strongs=H1350&t=KJV>.